whoopie pies

whoopie pies

Fun recipes for filled cookie cakes

Hannah Miles Photography by Steve Painter

RYLAND
PETERS
& SMALL

LONDON NEW YORK

conversion chart

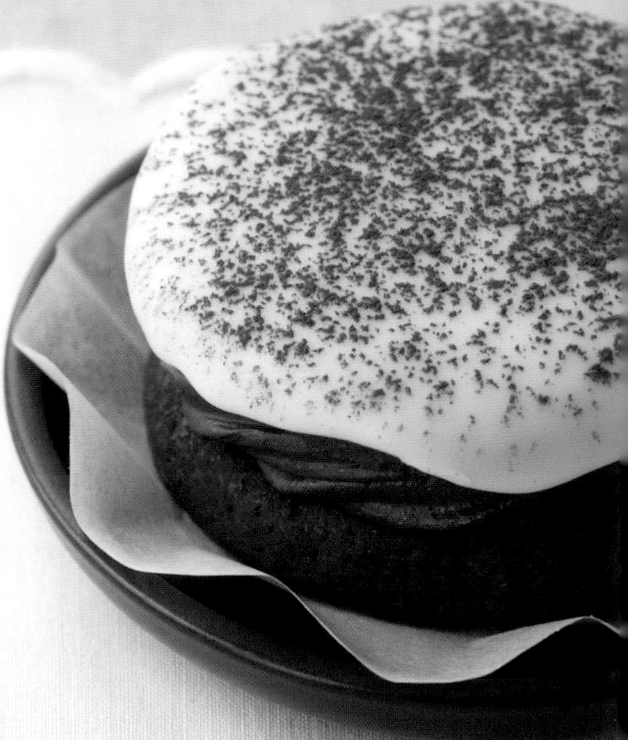

Volume equivalents:

American	Metric	Imperial
6 tbsp butter	85 g	3 oz.
7 tbsp butter	100 g	3½ oz.
1 stick butter	125 g	4½ oz.
1 teaspoon	5 ml	
1 tablespoon	15 ml	
¼ cup	60 ml	2 fl.oz.
⅓ cup	75 ml	2½ fl.oz.
½ cup	125 ml	4 fl.oz.
⅔ cup	150 ml	5 fl.oz. (¼ pint)
¾ cup	175 ml	6 fl.oz.
1 cup	250 ml	8 fl.oz.

Oven temperatures:

120°C/130°C	(250°F)	Gas ½
140°C	(275°F)	Gas 1
150°C	(300°F)	Gas 2
160°C/170°C	(325°F)	Gas 3
180°C	(350°F)	Gas 4
190°C	(375°F)	Gas 5
200°C	(400°F)	Gas 6
220°C	(425°F)	Gas 7

Weight equivalents:

Imperial	Metric
1 oz.	30 g
2 oz.	55 g
3 oz.	85 g
3½ oz.	100 g
4 oz.	115 g
5 oz.	140 g
6 oz.	175 g
8 oz. (½ lb.)	225 g
9 oz.	250 g
10 oz.	280 g
11½ oz.	325 g
12 oz.	350 g
13 oz.	375 g
14 oz.	400 g
15 oz.	425 g
16 oz. (1 lb.)	450 g

Measurements:

Inches	cm
¼ inch	0.5 cm
½ inch	1 cm
¾ inch	1.5 cm
1 inch	2.5 cm
2 inches	5 cm
3 inches	7 cm
4 inches	10 cm
5 inches	12 cm
6 inches	15 cm
7 inches	18 cm
8 inches	20 cm
9 inches	23 cm
10 inches	25 cm
11 inches	28 cm
12 inches	30 cm

To Ros, a much-missed friend and for her daughters Becca and Aimee.

Photography, design, and prop styling Steve Painter
Senior Commissioning Editor Julia Charles
Production Toby Marshall
Art Director Leslie Harrington
Publishing Director Alison Starling

Food Stylist Maxine Clark
Index Hilary Bird

First published in the United States in 2011 by Ryland Peters & Small, Inc.
519 Broadway, 5th Floor
New York, NY 10012
www.rylandpeters.com

10 9 8 7 6 5 4 3 2 1

Text © Hannah Miles 2011
Design and photographs
© Ryland Peters & Small 2011

Printed in China

ISBN: 978 1 84975 094 3

US Library of Congress cataloging-in-publication data has been applied for.

Notes
• All spoon measurements are level unless otherwise specified.
• When using the grated peel of lemons or limes in a recipe, try to find unwaxed fruits and wash well before using. If you can only find treated fruit, scrub well in warm soapy water and rinse before using.
• Ovens should be preheated to the specified temperatures. All ovens work slightly differently. If using a fan-assisted oven, follow the manufacturer's instructions for adjusting temperatures.
• Although whoopie pies can be made on cookies sheets, for best results we recommend a whoopie pie pan. These are available to but at www.williams-sonoma.com and from other retailers.

contents

6 introduction

8 classic pies

28 fruity pies

42 luxury pies

52 party pies

64 index

Making whoopie!

The whoopie pie is the ultimate sweet treat. Gone are the days of getting to the bottom of a cupcake with all the frosting already eaten. Whoopie pies are sandwiched together with creamy fillings and can be topped with frosting or a glaze which means that you can enjoy every mouthful. These yummy pies are perfect for coffee breaks, afternoon tea, parties, or celebrations—you can even create a whoopie pie wedding cake using the croquembouche recipe on page 56. Whoopie pies are not new and have been an American favorite for decades. The residents of Maine, Pennsylvania, and the Amish, all lay claim to the original whoopie, making it difficult to discover the whoopie's true origin, but I am happy to go with the theory that they were given their name by people "whooping" with delight when they discovered one in their lunch pack. I just love the idea of someone cheering for cake!

Whoopie pies are a cross between a cookie and a cake—softer than a chewy cookie but firmer than a pound cake. The basic ingredients can generally be found in any kitchen; if you do not have buttermilk in the fridge you can substitute plain yogurt, sour cream, or heavy cream mixed with the freshly squeezed juice of a lemon, for equally delicious results. Traditionally, whoopie pies are made with vegetable shortening (a solid white fat, such as Crisco) but having tested the recipes, I do prefer the flavor that butter gives to the pies. This is entirely a personal preference and you can use the more traditional shortening in the pie batter if you prefer. Let your imagination run wild with the color, flavorings, decorations, and sprinkles for these recipes. The whoopie batter takes color very well and a small spoon of food coloring paste gives great results.

6

There are several ways of baking the pies. Whoopie pie pans are available and are similar to cupcake pans. Each pan makes 12 pie halves and gives the perfect pie dome. If you do not have suitable pans, you can use two large cookie sheets lined with baking parchment or silicone mats. Either make mounds of mixture using an ice cream scoop or shape them with two spoons. For more regular shaped pies (or mini ones) spoon the mixture into a piping bag fitted with a large round nozzle and pipe 2½-inch diameter circles onto the cookie sheets. Whoopie pies are best eaten on the day they are made and recipes containing fresh cream must be refrigerated until you are ready to serve them.

There is something about whoopie pies, perhaps just even their name that just makes people smile. So why not whip up a batch today and spread a little happiness to those you love?

classic pies

classic whoopie pie

These chocolate and marshmallow pies are a true classic. Also known as "Gobs" or "Black and Whites", they have a rich chocolate flavor with a creamy marshmallow fluff filling. Sugary sweet and seriously addictive, I promise one bite and you will be hooked!

1 stick unsalted butter or vegetable shortening, softened

1 cup packed dark brown sugar

1 large egg

1 teaspoon vanilla extract

2 cups plus 2 tablespoons self-rising flour

⅓ cup cocoa powder

1 teaspoon baking powder

½ teaspoon salt

½ cup buttermilk

½ cup sour cream

⅓ cup hot (not boiling) water

Marshmallow fluff filling

7½-oz jar marshmallow fluff

1 stick unsalted butter, softened

1⅔ cups confectioners' sugar

1 teaspoon vanilla extract

3 tablespoons milk

two 12-hole whoopie pie pans, greased (optional)

a piping bag fitted with a large star nozzle (optional)

Makes 12

Preheat the oven to 350°F.

To make the pies, cream together the butter and brown sugar in a mixing bowl for 2–3 minutes using an electric handheld mixer, until light and creamy. Add the egg and vanilla extract and mix again. Sift the flour, cocoa, and baking powder into the bowl and add the salt, buttermilk, and sour cream. Whisk again until everything is incorporated. Add the hot water and whisk into the batter.

Put a large spoonful of batter into each hole in the prepared pans. (Alternatively, use 2 cookie sheets and follow the instructions given on page 7.) Leave to stand for 10 minutes then bake each pan in the preheated oven for 10–12 minutes. Remove from the oven, let cool slightly then turn out onto a wire rack to cool completely.

To make the filling, whisk together the marshmallow fluff and butter in a mixing bowl using an electric handheld mixer. Sift in the confectioners' sugar, add the vanilla extract and milk and whisk again for about 3–5 minutes, until light and creamy. Spoon the filling into the prepared piping bag and pipe a generous swirl of filling onto 12 of the whoopie pie halves. (If you do not have a piping bag, spread the filling over the pie halves with a round-bladed knife.) Top with the remaining pie halves and your whoopie pies are ready to enjoy.

red velvet pies

Red velvet cupcakes are an American favorite. The cake is flavored with cocoa and colored red, which gives the pies their distinctive look. Sandwiched together with a rich chocolate buttercream and topped with white chocolate, these whoopie pies are a chocoholic's delight!

1 stick unsalted butter or vegetable shortening, softened

1 cup granulated sugar

1 large egg

1 teaspoon vanilla extract

2⅓ cups self-rising flour

2½ tablespoons cocoa powder

1 teaspoon baking powder

½ teaspoon salt

1 cup buttermilk

2 teaspoons red food colouring paste

⅓ cup hot (not boiling) water

Chocolate buttercream

9 oz. bittersweet chocolate

1 stick plus 3 tablespoons unsalted butter

1 cup confectioners' sugar

To decorate

10 oz. white chocolate, melted

cocoa powder, to dust

two 12-hole whoopie pie pans, greased (optional)

a piping bag fitted with a large star nozzle (optional)

Makes 12

Preheat the oven to 350°F.

To make the pies, cream together the butter and sugar in a mixing bowl for 2–3 minutes using an electric handheld mixer, until light and creamy. Add the egg and vanilla extract and mix again. Sift the flour, cocoa, and baking powder into the bowl and add the salt, buttermilk, and the red food colouring paste. Whisk again until everything is incorporated. Add the hot water and whisk into the batter.

Put a large spoonful of batter into each hole in the prepared pans. (Alternatively, use 2 cookie sheets and follow the instructions given on page 7.) Leave to stand for 10 minutes then bake each pan in the preheated oven for 10–12 minutes. Remove from the oven, let cool slightly then turn out onto a wire rack to cool completely.

To make the chocolate buttercream, break the chocolate into pieces and place in a heatproof bowl set on top of a saucepan of barely simmering water. Take care the base of the bowl does not touch the water. Stir until the chocolate has melted. Let the chocolate cool, then whisk together with the butter and confectioners' sugar using an electric whisk. Spoon the buttercream into the prepared piping bag and pipe a generous swirl of buttercream onto 12 of the whoopie pie halves. (If you do not have a piping bag, spread the buttercream over the pie halves with a round-bladed knife.)

To decorate the pie tops, take the remaining pie halves and put them on a sheet of baking parchment. Melt the white chocolate following the method given above. Spoon melted chocolate over each one, sufficient to drizzle over the sides. Set aside to set.

Top the buttercream-topped pie halves with the white chocolate-topped pie halves, dust with cocoa powder and your whoopie pies are ready to enjoy.

vanilla dream

Victoria sandwich cake is an English classic and much-loved teatime treat. Here, light and fluffy vanilla sponge cakes are filled with a delicate buttercream and raspberry preserve to make dainty little pies that are just perfect.

1 stick unsalted butter or vegetable shortening, softened

1 cup granulated sugar

1 large egg

1 teaspoon vanilla extract

2½ cups self-rising flour

1 teaspoon baking powder

½ teaspoon salt

½ cup buttermilk

⅓ cup sour cream

⅓ cup hot (not boiling) water

Vanilla buttercream

6 tablespoons unsalted butter, softened

3 cups confectioners' sugar, sifted

1 teaspoon vanilla extract

3 tablespoons milk

4 tablespoons raspberry preserve

confectioners' sugar, to dust

two 12-hole whoopie pie pans, greased (optional)

a piping bag fitted with a large star nozzle (optional)

Makes 12

Preheat the oven to 350°F.

To make the pies, cream together the butter and sugar in a mixing bowl for 2–3 minutes using an electric handheld mixer, until light and creamy. Add the egg and vanilla extract and mix again. Sift the flour and baking powder into the bowl and add the salt, buttermilk, and sour cream. Whisk again until everything is incorporated. Add the hot water and whisk into the batter.

Put a large spoonful of batter into each hole in the prepared pans. (Alternatively, use 2 cookies sheets and follow the instructions given on page 7.) Leave to stand for 10 minutes then bake the pies in the preheated oven for 10–12 minutes. Remove from the oven, let cool slightly then turn out onto a wire rack to cool completely.

To make the vanilla buttercream, whisk the butter, confectioners' sugar, vanilla extract, and milk together in a bowl for 2–3 minutes, until light and creamy. Spoon the buttercream into the prepared piping bag and pipe a swirl of filling onto 12 of the whoopie pie halves. (If you do not have a piping bag, spread the filling over the pie halves with a round-bladed knife.) Put a teaspoon of raspberry preserve on top of the buttercream. Top with the remaining pie halves, dust liberally with confectioners' sugar and your whoopie pies are ready to enjoy.

mocha pies

These mocha coffee pies give you the ultimate chocolate, caffeine, and sugar hit. It works on so many levels—waking you up and making you feel happy!

1 stick unsalted butter or vegetable shortening, softened

½ cup packed dark brown sugar

½ packed light brown sugar

1 large egg

1 teaspoon vanilla extract

2 cups plus 2 tablespoons self-rising flour

⅓ cup cocoa powder

1 teaspoon baking powder

⅓ teaspoon salt

1 cup sour cream

1 tablespoon instant coffee, dissolved in a scant ⅓ cup hot water

⅔ cup semisweet chocolate chips

Coffee mousse filling

1 tablespoon instant coffee

7 oz. white chocolate

3½ oz. semisweet chocolate

1¼ cups heavy cream

Coffee glacé icing

1 tablespoon instant coffee

1⅜ cups confectioners' sugar

To decorate

white chocolate curls

12 chocolate coffee beans

two 12-hole whoopie pie pans, greased (optional)

a piping bag fitted with a large round nozzle (optional)

Makes 12

Preheat the oven to 350ºF.

To make the pies, cream together the butter and brown sugars in a mixing bowl for 2–3 minutes using an electric handheld mixer, until light and creamy. Add the egg and vanilla extract and mix again. Sift the flour, cocoa, and baking powder into the bowl and add the salt and sour cream. Whisk again until everything is incorporated. Add the dissolved coffee and whisk into the batter. Stir in the chocolate chips.

Put a large spoonful of mixture into each hole in the prepared pans. (Alternatively, use 2 cookie sheets and follow the instructions given on page 7.) Leave to stand for 10 minutes then bake each pan in the preheated oven for 10–12 minutes. Remove from the oven, let cool slightly then turn out onto a wire rack to cool.

To make the coffee mousse filling, dissolve the coffee in 1 tablespoon hot water. Melt the white and semisweet chocolates following the method given on page 10 and leave to cool. Whip the heavy cream to stiff peaks then fold in the melted chocolates and dissolved coffee. Cover and chill in the fridge for 1 hour.

To make the coffee icing, dissolve the coffee in 1 tablespoon hot water and let cool. Add the cooled coffee to the confectioners' sugar and mix with 1–2 tablespoons cold water until you have a smooth icing. Spread over 12 of the pie halves, sprinkle with chocolate curls, and finish each one with a chocolate coffee bean in the center and let the icing set.

Spoon the chilled coffee mousse filling into the prepared piping bag and pipe circles of mousse onto the remaining pies halves. (If you do not have a piping bag, spread the filling over the pie halves with a round-bladed knife.) Top with the decorated pie halves and your whoopie pies are ready to enjoy.

pumpkin pies

Warm, buttery, spiced pumpkin pie is a classic fall treat. Decorated as cute pumpkins, these whoopie pies make a perfect halloween or Thanksgiving treat for kids and adults alike!

1 stick unsalted butter or vegetable shortening, softened

1 cup packed dark brown sugar

1 large egg

⅔ cup canned pumpkin purée (such as Libby's)

2⅔ cups self-rising flour

2 teaspoons ground cinnamon

1 teaspoon apple pie spice

1 teaspoon ground ginger

1 teaspoon baking powder

½ teaspoon salt

1 cup plain yogurt

⅓ cup hot (not boiling) water

Cream cheese filling

7 oz. cream cheese

1 stick unsalted butter, softened

3¼ cups confectioners' sugar

Orange glacé icing

1⅔ cups confectioners' sugar

juice of 1 small orange

orange food coloring

To decorate

3 heaping tablespoons confectioners' sugar

red and green food coloring

2 chocolate sticks

two 12-hole whoopie pie pans, greased (optional)

three piping bags, a small round hole nozzle, a large star nozzle and a leaf nozzle

Makes 12

Preheat the oven to 350°F.

To make the pies, cream together the butter and brown sugar in a mixing bowl for 2–3 minutes using an electric handheld mixer, until light and creamy. Add the egg and pumpkin purée and mix again. Sift the flour, cinnamon, apple pie spice, ginger, and baking powder into the bowl and add the salt and yogurt. Whisk until everything is incorporated. Add the hot water and whisk into the batter.

Put a large spoonful of batter into each hole in the prepared pans. (Alternatively, use 2 cookie sheets and follow the instructions given on page 7.) Leave to stand for 10 minutes then bake each pan in the preheated oven for 10–12 minutes. Remove from the oven, let cool slightly then turn out onto a wire rack to cool completely.

To make the cream cheese filling, whisk together the cream cheese, butter, and confectioners' sugar until light and creamy. Remove 4 tablespoons of the mixture, mix in a drop of green food coloring and set aside as this will be used later for decoration. Spoon the remaining filling into a piping bag fitted with the large star nozzle and pipe a generous swirl of filling onto 12 of the pies halves. Set aside.

To make the orange glacé icing, mix together the confectioners' sugar, orange juice, and a few drops of orange food coloring until you have smooth glossy icing. Cover the remaining pie halves with the icing using a round-bladed knife and leave to set. When the icing has set, mix 3 tablespoons of icing sugar with 1–2 teaspoons cold water and a few drop of orange and red food coloring to make a thick, darker orange icing. Spoon the icing into a piping bag fitted with a small round hole nozzle and pipe 5 lines from the center of each pie (to resemble the lines on a pumpkin). Spoon the green cream cheese filling into a clean piping bag fitted with a leaf nozzle and pipe green leaves and a curly stem on top of each pie, as shown. Cut each chocolate stick into 6 pieces and put in the center to look like stalks.

Top the cream cheese filling-topped pie halves with the decorated pie halves and your whoopie pies are ready to enjoy.

peanut butter and jelly pies

1 stick unsalted butter or vegetable shortening, softened

1 tablespoon smooth peanut butter

1 cup granulated sugar

1 large egg

2⅓ cups self-rising flour

1 teaspoon baking powder

½ teaspoon salt

1 cup buttermilk

⅓ cup hot (not boiling) water

Peanut glaze

1 tablespoon unsalted butter

1 tablespoon smooth peanut butter

1¼ cups confectioners' sugar

⅓ cup salted peanuts, chopped

Filling

5 tablespoons soft unsalted butter

2 tablespoons smooth peanut butter

1⅔ cups confectioners' sugar

3 tablespoons sour cream

3 tablespoons raspberry jelly

two 12-hole whoopie pie pans, greased (optional)
a piping bag fitted with a large star nozzle (optional)

Makes 12

Peanut butter and jelly sandwiches are an all-time classic—the saltiness of peanuts and sweetness of the jelly providing the ultimate sweet and savory combination.

Preheat the oven to 350°F.

To make the pies, cream together the butter, peanut butter, and sugar in a mixing bowl for 2–3 minutes using an electric handheld mixer, until light and creamy. Add the egg and mix again. Sift the flour and baking powder into the bowl and add the salt and buttermilk. Whisk again until everything is incorporated. Add the hot water and whisk into the batter.

Put a large spoonful of batter into each hole in the prepared pans. (Alternatively, use 2 cookie sheets and follow the instructions given on page 7.) Leave to stand for 10 minutes then bake each pan in the preheated oven for 10–12 minutes. Remove from the oven, let cool slightly then turn out onto a wire rack.

To make the peanut glaze, heat the butter, peanut butter, confectioners' sugar, and ¼ cup cold water in a saucepan set over low heat. Simmer until you have a smooth thick glaze, then spoon this over half of the pie halves. This is best done whilst the pies are still warm on the wire rack and with baking parchment underneath to catch any drips. Leave to cool completely.

To make the filling, whisk together the butter, peanut butter, icing sugar and soured cream in a mixing bowl using an electric handheld mixer, until light and creamy. Spoon the filling into the prepared piping bag and pipe stars of filling in a ring onto the 12 unglazed pie halves – reserving a little to decorate. (If you do not have a piping bag, thickly spread the filling over the pie halves thickly with a round-bladed knife.) Put a spoonful of jam on top of the filling and top with the glazed pie halves. Pipe a star of the reserved filling on top of each one and sprinkle with the chopped peanuts. Your whoopie pies are ready to enjoy.

mini pistachio pies

There are few things more therapeutic than popping pistachios from their shells and eating them—their exotic taste, transporting you to the Middle East, as does this irresistible little pie.

1 stick unsalted butter or vegetable shortening, softened

1 cup granulated sugar

1 large egg

1 teaspoon vanilla extract

2½ cups self-rising flour

1 teaspoon baking powder

½ teaspoon salt

1 cup plain yogurt

⅔ cup shelled pistachios, finely chopped

a few drops of green food coloring

⅓ cup hot (not boiling) water

Meringue filling

2 egg whites

½ cup superfine sugar

5 tablespoons unsalted butter, melted

⅔ cup shelled pistachios, finely ground

To decorate

1⅔ confectioners' sugar

a few drops of green food coloring

2 tablespoons chopped pistachios

two cookie sheets, lined with baking parchment or silicone mats

a piping bag fitted with a large round nozzle (optional)

Makes 24

Preheat the oven to 350°F.

To make the pies, cream together the butter and sugar in a mixing bowl for 2–3 minutes using an electric handheld mixer, until light and creamy. Add the egg and vanilla extract and mix again. Sift the flour and baking powder into the bowl and add the salt, yogurt, pistachios, and food coloring. Whisk again until everything is incorporated. Add the hot water and whisk into the batter.

Spoon the batter into the prepared piping bag and pipe 48 rounds on the prepared cookie sheets (about 1-inch diameter) leaving a gap between each one as they will spread during baking. Alternatively, use 2 teaspoons to form small rounds directly onto the sheets. Leave to stand for 10 minutes then bake each sheet in the preheated oven for 10–12 minutes. Remove from the oven, let cool slightly then transfer to a wire rack to cool.

To make the meringue filling, put the egg whites and superfine sugar in a heatproof bowl set over a saucepan of simmering water, making sure that the bowl does not touch the water. Whisk continuously for 2–3 minutes, until the sugar has dissolved. Remove the bowl from the heat and whisk for 2–3 minutes more, until the meringue forms stiff peaks. Drizzle the melted butter into the meringue whilst still whisking. Fold in the pistachios and chill in the fridge for 3–4 hours.

To decorate, mix the confectioners' sugar and food coloring with 2–3 tablespoons cold water. Spread over 24 of the pie halves and sprinkle with pistachios. Spoon the meringue onto the un-iced halves, top with the iced halves and your whoopie pies are ready to enjoy.

cookies and cream pies

Chocolate and vanilla Oreo cookies dunked in milk are such a treat. Although you can't quite dunk these little pies, they are delicious washed down with a glass of ice-cold milk.

1 stick unsalted butter or vegetable shortening, softened

1 cup packed dark brown sugar

1 large egg

1 teaspoon vanilla extract

2 cups plus 2 tablespoons self-rising flour

⅓ cup cocoa powder

1 teaspoon baking powder

½ teaspoon salt

½ cup sour cream

½ cup buttermilk

⅓ cup hot (not boiling) water

Cookie crumb filling

6 tablespoons soft unsalted butter

3 cups confectioners' sugar, sifted

1 teaspoon vanilla extract

¼ cup milk

1 tablespoon cocoa powder, sifted

2 oz. Oreo cookies, or similar

To decorate

5½ oz. white chocolate

12 mini Oreo cookies, or similar

two 12-hole whoopie pie pans, greased (optional)

a piping bag fitted with a large star nozzle (optional)

Makes 12

Preheat the oven to 350ºF.

To make the pies, cream together the butter and brown sugar in a mixing bowl for 2–3 minutes using an electric handheld mixer, until light and creamy. Add the egg and vanilla extract and mix again. Sift the flour, cocoa, and baking powder into the bowl and add the salt, sour cream, and buttermilk. Whisk again until everything is incorporated. Add the hot water and whisk into the batter.

Put a large spoonful of mixture into each hole in the prepared pans. (Alternatively, use 2 cookie sheets and follow the instructions given on page 7.) Leave to stand for 10 minutes then bake each pan in the preheated oven for 10–12 minutes. Remove from the oven, let cool slightly then turn out onto a wire rack to cool completely.

To decorate, melt the white chocolate following the instructions on page 10, then using a round-bladed knife spread a chocolate semi-circle over 12 of the pie halves. Leave to set.

To make the cookie crumb filling, whisk together the butter, confectioners' sugar, vanilla extract, and 3 tablespoons of the milk in a bowl using an electric handheld mixer, until light and creamy. Remove 2 tablespoons of the buttercream, whisk the cocoa powder into it and set aside to decorate. Blitz the cookies in a food processor to a fine powder. Fold the cookie crumbs and the remaining 1 tablespoon of milk into the remaining buttercream.

Spoon some cookie crumb filling onto the undecorated pie halves and spread thickly with a round-bladed knife. Top each one with a white chocolate-decorated pie half. Put the reserved chocolate buttercream in the prepared piping bag and pipe a star into the center of each pie. (If you do not have a piping bag, simply use a teaspoon.) Top with a mini Oreo cookie and your whoopie pies are ready to enjoy.

pecan pies

Mouthwatering pecan pie, with its buttery toffee caramel and crunchy nuts, is the inspiration for these, my favorite pies. The filling is made with a pecan praline which has a deliciously sweet and nutty caramel flavor.

1 stick unsalted butter or vegetable shortening, softened

1 cup packed dark brown sugar

1 large egg

1 tablespoon pure maple syrup

2⅓ cups self-rising flour

1 teaspoon baking powder

½ teaspoon salt

1 cup sour cream

⅓ cup hot (not boiling) water

Maple glaze

⅓ cup packed dark brown sugar

¾ cup pure maple syrup

2 tablespoons corn syrup

2 tablespoons unsalted butter

Praline cream filling

½ cup pecans

½ cup granulated sugar

1¼ cups heavy cream, whipped to stiff peaks

two 12-hole whoopie pie pans, greased (optional)

a piping bag fitted with a large round nozzle (optional)

Makes 12

Preheat the oven to 350°F.

To make the pies, cream together the butter and brown sugar in a mixing bowl for 2–3 minutes using an electric handheld mixer, until light and creamy. Add the egg and maple syrup and mix again. Sift the flour and baking powder into the bowl and add the salt and sour cream. Whisk again until everything is incorporated. Add the hot water and whisk into the batter.

Put a large spoonful of batter into each hole in the prepared pans. (Alternatively, use 2 cookie sheets and follow the instructions given on page 7.) Leave to stand for 10 minutes then bake each pan in the preheated oven for 10–12 minutes. Remove from the oven, let cool slightly then turn out onto a wire rack.

To make the maple glaze, put the sugar, maple syrup, corn syrup, and butter in a saucepan set over gentle heat and warm until the sugar has melted. Drizzle over 12 of the pie halves. This is best done whilst the pies are still warm and on the wire rack, with baking parchment underneath to catch any drips. Leave to cool completely

To make the praline cream filling, sprinkle the pecans over a sheet of baking parchment, selecting 12 halves to use for decoration. Warm the sugar in a saucepan set over gentle heat, until melted and golden. Do not stir but watch very closely as it will burn easily. As the sugar starts to melt, swirl the pan. When melted, use a spoon to drizzle the caramel over all of the pecans, swirling lacy patterns over the pecans selected for decoration. Once cooled, set the decoration pecans to one side and blitz the remaining ones to a fine dust in a food processor. Fold this praline powder into the whipped cream. Spoon the cream into the prepared piping bag and pipe circles of it onto the unglazed pie halves. (If you do not have a piping bag, spread the filling over the pie halves with a round-bladed knife.) Top with the glazed pie halves and finish each one with a caramel pecan. Your whoopie pies are ready to enjoy.

caramel popcorn pies

I just adore the complete "kitschness" of these pies, with a caramel glaze and piled high with popcorn. They would be absolutely perfect to serve for a movie night at home.

1 cup granulated sugar
½ teaspoon sea salt flakes
1 stick unsalted butter or vegetable shortening, softened
1 large egg
2⅓ cups self-rising flour
1 teaspoon baking powder
1 cup buttermilk

Salted caramel sauce
½ stick unsalted butter
¼ cup packed dark brown sugar
1 tablespoon pure maple syrup
a pinch of salt
1 tablespoon heavy cream

Caramel glaze
¾ cup confectioners' sugar
1 tablespoon salted caramel sauce (see above)
½ cup toffee popcorn, to decorate
sugar stars, to sprinkle

Caramel filling
2¾ cups confectioners' sugar
1 tablespoon milk
5 tablespoons soft unsalted butter

two 12-hole whoopie pie pans, greased (optional)
a piping bag fitted with a large star nozzle (optional)

Makes 12

Preheat the oven to 350°F.

To make the pies, gently heat ½ cup sugar in a saucepan, until melted and light golden. Do not stir the sugar whilst it is melting but watch very closely as it will burn easily. As it starts to melt, swirl the pan and when melted, carefully add ⅓ cup cold water. Continue to heat until the sugar dissolves in the water and then add the salt. Cream together the butter and the remaining sugar in a mixing bowl using an electric handheld mixer, until light and creamy. Add the egg and mix. Sift the flour and baking powder into the bowl and add the buttermilk. Mix until incorporated. Reheat the salted caramel water until hot and whisk into the batter.

Put a large spoonful of batter into each hole in the prepared pans. (Alternatively, use 2 cookie sheets and follow the instructions given on page 7.) Leave to stand for 10 minutes then bake each pan in the preheated oven for 10–12 minutes. Remove from the oven, let cool slightly then turn out onto a wire rack.

To make the salted caramel sauce, put the butter, brown sugar, maple syrup, and salt in a saucepan and warm over gentle heat, until the sugar has dissolved. Add the cream to the pan and heat for a few minutes more. Set aside.

To make the caramel glaze, put the confectioners' sugar, 1 tablespoon of the salted caramel sauce, and 2 tablespoons cold water in a saucepan. Warm over gentle heat until the sugar has dissolved. Spoon the glaze over 12 of the pie halves, wait a few minutes and spoon over a second coat. This is best done whilst the pies are still warm and on the wire rack, with baking parchment underneath to catch any drips. Pile pieces of popcorn on top of the glaze and sprinkle with sugar stars. Leave to set.

To make the caramel filling, whisk together the confectioners' sugar, milk, butter, and remaining salted caramel sauce in a bowl, until light and creamy. Spoon into the prepared piping bag and pipe a swirl onto the unglazed pie halves. (If you do not have a piping bag, spread the filling over the pie halves with a round-bladed knife.) Top with the popcorn-decorated pie halves and your whoopie pies are ready to enjoy.

fruity pies

chocolate and cherry pies

These indulgent pies are inspired by the classic Black Forest gateaux from Germany—a heady combination of cherries, chocolate, and kirsch. For an alcohol-free version omit the kirsch.

3 oz. semisweet chocolate

1 stick unsalted butter or vegetable shortening, softened

1 cup packed dark brown sugar

1 large egg

2¼ cups plus 2 tablespoons self-rising flour

2½ tablespoons cocoa powder

1 teaspoon baking powder

½ teaspoon salt

1 cup plain yogurt

⅓ cup hot (not boiling) water

Cherry cream filling

1 cup fresh cherries, pitted

2 tablespoons granulated sugar

2 tablespoons kirsch (optional)

1½ cups heavy cream, whipped

Chocolate glaze

3 tablespoons unsalted butter

⅓ cup light corn syrup

3½ oz. semisweet chocolate, broken into pieces

12 fresh cherries with stalks on, to decorate

two 12-hole whoopie pie pans, greased (optional)

Makes 12

Preheat the oven to 350°F.

To make the pies, first melt the semisweet chocolate following the instructions given on page 10. Cream together the butter and brown sugar in a mixing bowl for 2–3 minutes using an electric handheld mixer, until light and creamy. Add the egg and mix again. Sift the flour, cocoa, and baking powder into the bowl and add the salt, melted chocolate, and yogurt. Whisk again until everything is incorporated. Add the hot water and whisk into the batter.

Put a large spoonful of batter into each hole in the prepared pans. (Alternatively, use 2 cookie sheets and follow the instructions given on page 7.) Leave to stand for 10 minutes then bake each pan for 10–12 minutes in the preheated oven. Remove from the oven, let cool slightly then turn out onto a wire rack.

To make the cherry cream filling, put the cherries in a saucepan with the sugar and ⅓ cup cold water. Simmer over low heat until soft, then remove from the heat. Stir in the kirsch (if using) and set aside to cool. When cooled, fold the cherry compote into the whipped cream, cover and chill in the fridge until needed.

To make the chocolate glaze, heat the butter with the corn syrup, chocolate, and 2½ tablespoons cold water in a saucepan, until the chocolate and butter have melted and you have a shiny syrup. Spoon the glaze over 12 of the pie halves. This is best done whilst the pies are still warm and on the wire rack and with baking parchment underneath to catch any drips. Top each one with a fresh cherry and allow to set.

Spoon some cherry cream filling onto the unglazed pie halves and spread with a round-bladed-knife. Top each one with a glazed and cherry-topped pie half and your whoopie pies are ready to enjoy.

strawberry cream pies

Strawberries and cream—the epitome of British summertime. Tennis at Wimbledon, picking ripe berries at fruit farms and making homemade strawberry preserve. These pies are reminiscent of a classic scone, served with clotted cream and strawberry preserve.

1 stick unsalted butter or vegetable shortening, softened

1 cup granulated sugar

1 large egg

1 teaspoon vanilla extract

2 teaspoons rose syrup or rose water

2½ cups self-rising flour

1 teaspoon baking powder

½ teaspoon salt

½ cup buttermilk

½ cup plain yogurt

⅓ cup hot (not boiling) water

Strawberry cream filling

3 cups fresh strawberries

10 oz. clotted cream or whipped heavy cream

4 tablespoons strawberry preserve

confectioners' sugar, to dust

two 12-hole whoopie pie pans, greased (optional)

Makes 12

Preheat the oven to 350°F.

To make the pies, cream together the butter and sugar in a mixing bowl for 2–3 minutes using an electric handheld mixer, until light and creamy. Add the egg, vanilla extract, and rose syrup and mix again. Sift the flour and baking powder into the bowl and add the salt, buttermilk, and yogurt. Whisk again until everything is incorporated. Add the hot water and whisk into the batter.

Put a large spoonful of batter into each hole in the prepared pans. (Alternatively, use 2 cookie sheets and follow the instructions given on page 7.) Leave to stand for 10 minutes then bake each pan in the preheated oven for 10–12 minutes. Remove from the oven, cool slightly then turn out onto a wire rack to cool completely.

To make the strawberry cream filling, remove the hulls and cut the strawberries into slices with a sharp knife. Place a spoonful of clotted cream onto 12 of the pie halves, top each with a teaspoon of strawberry preserve and some strawberry slices. Put a remaining pie half on top of each one, dust liberally with confectioners' sugar and your whoopie pies are ready to enjoy.

apple crumble pies

1 stick unsalted butter or vegetable shortening, softened
½ cup granulated sugar
½ cup packed dark brown sugar
1 large egg
1 teaspoon ground cinnamon
2½ cups self-rising flour
1 teaspoon baking powder
½ teaspoon salt
1 cup buttermilk
⅓ cup hot (not boiling) water

Apple filling

2 large cooking apples
¼ cup dark soft brown sugar
1 tablespoon unsalted butter
1 teaspoon ground cinnamon
1 tablespoon light corn syrup

Crumble topping

5 tablespoons self-rising flour
3 tablespoons cold unsalted butter
2½ tablespoons granulated sugar

Custard filling

7 oz. white chocolate
¾ cup heavy cream, whipped
6 oz. prepared vanilla pudding

two 12-hole whoopie pie pans, greased (optional)

Makes 12

Buttery crumble-topped pies filled with a rich vanilla custard and baked apple slices, these pies are completely delicious. For an extra special treat, why not serve them for dessert with a pitcher of cream on the side for the ultimate in comfort food.

Preheat the oven to 350°F.

To make the apple filling, peel, core, and thinly slice the apples. Put them in an ovenproof dish and top with the brown sugar, butter, cinnamon, corn syrup, and 1 tablespoon cold water. Bake in the preheated oven for 20–25 minutes, until the apple slices are soft but still hold their shape. Set aside to cool. Leave the oven on.

To make the pies, cream together the butter and granulated and brown sugars in a mixing bowl for 2–3 minutes using an electric handheld mixer, until light and creamy. Add the egg and cinnamon and mix again. Sift the flour and baking powder into the bowl and add the salt and buttermilk. Whisk again until everything is incorporated. Add the hot water and whisk into the batter.

Put a large spoonful of batter into each hole in the prepared pans. (Alternatively, use 2 cookie sheets and follow the instructions given on page 7.) Leave to stand for 10 minutes. Meanwhile, make the crumble topping. Put the flour in a bowl and using your fingertips rub in the butter then stir in the sugar. Bake the pies in the still-hot oven for 5 minutes, then sprinkle the crumble topping over 12 of the pie halves and bake for a further 5–7 minutes, until golden. Remove the pies from the oven, let cool slightly then turn out onto a wire rack to cool completely.

To make the custard filling, melt the white chocolate following the method given on page 10 and let cool. Gently fold the whipped cream into the vanilla pudding, along with the melted chocolate. Chill in the fridge for 1–2 hours, then spoon a little custard filling over the pie halves which do not have crumble topping on. Drain the baked apples and put a spoonful on top of the filling. Top with the crumble pie halves and your whoopie pies are ready to enjoy.

lemon sherbet pies

Sherbet lemons are a childhood favorite—sharp lemon candies with a fizzy treat when you get to the center. These zingy and zesty pies are just as delicious, with their luscious lemon curd and cream cheese filling and fun sherbet decoration.

1 stick unsalted butter or vegetable shortening, softened

1 cup granulated sugar

1 large egg

finely grated peel of 2 lemons

2½ cups self-rising flour

1 teaspoon baking powder

½ teaspoon salt

1 cup buttermilk

⅓ cup hot (not boiling) water

Lemon glacé icing

1⅔ cups confectioners' sugar

2–3 tablespoons lemon juice

Cream cheese filling

7 oz. cream cheese

2 tablespoons lemon curd

1 tablespoon confectioners' sugar, sifted

To decorate

lemon-flavored sherbet crystals

12 mini lemon jelly slices

two 12-hole whoopie pie pans, greased (optional)

a piping bag fitted with a large round nozzle (optional)

Makes 12

Preheat the oven to 350°F.

To make the pies, cream together the butter and sugar in a mixing bowl for 2–3 minutes using an electric handheld mixer, until light and creamy. Add the egg and grated lemon peel and mix again. Sift the flour and baking powder into the bowl and add the salt and buttermilk. Whisk again until everything is incorporated. Add the hot water and whisk into the batter.

Put a large spoonful of batter into each hole in the prepared pans. (Alternatively, use 2 cookie sheets and follow the instructions given on page 7.) Leave to stand for 10 minutes then bake each pan in the preheated oven for 10–12 minutes. Remove from the oven, let cool slightly then turn out onto a wire rack to cool completely.

To make the lemon icing, mix together the icing sugar and lemon juice in a bowl, until it forms a smooth paste. Spread the icing over half of the pie halves and decorate each with a sprinkle of sherbet crystals and a lemon jelly slice.

To make the cream cheese filling, whisk the cream cheese until fluffy and fold in the lemon curd and confectioners' sugar. Put the filling in the prepared piping bag and pipe blobs of filling onto the un-iced pie halves. (If you do not have a piping bag, spread the filling over the pie halves with a round-bladed knife.) Top each one with an iced and decorated pie half and your whoopie pies are ready to enjoy.

key lime jello pies

The tangy citrus jello filling actually makes these pies wobble—the children who tried them when we tested the recipe loved them and they would be perfect for a kid's party.

1 stick unsalted butter or vegetable shortening, softened

1 cup granulated sugar

1 large egg

finely grated peel of 2 limes

2½ cups self-rising flour

1 teaspoon baking powder

½ teaspoon salt

1 cup buttermilk

⅓ cup hot (not boiling) water

Lime jello filling

4 leaves of gelatin

7 oz. cream cheese

1¼ cups sour cream

1 cup granulated sugar

freshly squeezed juice of 1 orange and 1 lemon

finely grated peel and freshly squeezed juice of 2 limes

a few drops of green food coloring

Lime glacé icing

1⅔ cups confectioners' sugar

2–3 tablespoons lime juice

a few drops green food coloring

50 mini lime jelly slices, chopped

two 12-hole whoopie pie pans, greased (optional)

a piping bag fitted with a large star nozzle (optional)

Makes 12

Begin by preparing the lime jello filling as this will need to set in the fridge for several hours. Soak the gelatine leaves in cold water for about 5 minutes. Put the cream cheese, sour cream, and sugar in a blender and whizz until mixed. Put the orange, lemon, and lime juices and gelatin in a saucepan and heat over very gentle heat until the gelatin has all dissolved. Do not allow it to reach a boil otherwise the gelatin will lose its setting properties. Pour the citrus juice through a strainer into the blender, add the grated lime peel and a few drops of green food coloring and mix again. Transfer to a bowl and allow to set in the fridge for about 2–3 hours.

Preheat the oven to 350°F. To make the pies, cream together the butter and sugar in a mixing bowl for 2–3 minutes using an electric handheld mixer, until light and creamy. Add the egg and grated lime peel and mix again. Sift the flour and baking powder into the bowl and add the salt and buttermilk. Whisk again until everything is incorporated. Add the hot water and whisk into the batter.

Put a large spoonful of batter into each hole in the prepared pans. (Alternatively, use 2 cookie sheets and follow the instructions given on page 7.) Leave to stand for 10 minutes then bake each pan in the preheated oven for 10–12 minutes. Remove from the oven, let cool slightly then turn out onto a wire rack to cool completely.

To make the lime icing, mix together the confectioners' sugar, lime juice, and food coloring until it forms a smooth paste. Spread a little over 12 of the pie halves and top with the chopped lime jelly slices. Leave to set. Spoon the lime jello filling into the prepared piping bag and pipe a swirl of filling onto the un-iced pie halves. (If you do not have a piping bag, spread the filling over the pie halves with a round-bladed knife.) Top each with a decorated pie half and your whoopie pies are ready to enjoy.

Chambord raspberry pies

Raspberries picked straight from the bushes on my mum's allotment are a much anticipated summer treat. Chambord (a raspberry liqueur beautifully presented in a gilded bottle) is delicious with Prosecco or Champagne but I have used it here, in both the glaze and the sumptuous cream filling, to enhance the "raspberriness" of these luxurious pies.

1 stick unsalted butter or vegetable shortening, softened

1 cup granulated sugar

1 large egg

1 teaspoon vanilla extract

2⅓ cups self-rising flour

1 teaspoon baking powder

½ teaspoon salt

1 cup buttermilk

⅓ cup hot (not boiling) water

Raspberry cream filling

⅔ cup heavy cream

1 cup mascarpone cheese

2 tablespoons Chambord liqueur

½ cup fresh raspberries

Chambord glaze

3 tablespoons confectioners' sugar

2 tablespoons Chambord liqueur

To decorate

12 fresh raspberries

gold leaf (optional)

two 12-hole whoopie pie pans, greased (optional)

a piping bag fitted with a large star nozzle (optional)

Makes 12

Preheat the oven to 350ºF.

To make the pies, cream together the butter and sugar in a mixing bowl for 2–3 minutes using an electric handheld mixer, until light and creamy. Add the egg and vanilla extract and mix again. Sift the flour and baking powder into the bowl and add the salt and buttermilk. Whisk again until everything is incorporated. Add the hot water and whisk into the batter.

Put a large spoonful of batter into each hole in the prepared pans. (Alternatively, use 2 cookie sheets and follow the instructions given on page 7.) Leave to stand for 10 minutes then bake each pan in the preheated oven for 10–12 minutes. Remove from the oven, let cool slightly then turn out onto a wire rack to cool completely.

To make the raspberry cream filling, whip the heavy cream to stiff peaks. Beat the mascarpone and then whisk it into the cream along with the liqueur and the raspberries. The raspberries will crush as you mix them. Chill in the fridge until you are ready to assemble the pies.

To make the glaze, put the confectioners' sugar, liqueur, and 1 tablespoon cold water in a small saucepan and heat until the confectioners' sugar has dissolved. Drizzle the glaze over 12 of the pie halves and top each one with a raspberry. Brush the raspberries with a little of the glaze using a paint brush and press on the gold leaf (if using) with tweezers or the tip of a sharp knife. Spoon the chilled filling into the prepared piping bag and pipe stars of the filling onto the unglazed pie halves. (If you do not have a piping bag, spread the filling over the pie halves with a round-bladed knife.) Top each one with a decorated pie half and your whoopie pies are ready to enjoy.

banoffee pies

Rich caramel-smothered bananas, sandwiched between banana-flavored pies with fresh cream, make these pies a banoffee lover's delight. Make sure that you use really ripe bananas for a "true" banana flavor.

1 very ripe banana

freshly squeezed juice of ½ a lemon

1 stick unsalted butter or vegetable shortening, softened

1 cup granulated sugar

1 large egg

2½ cups self-rising flour

1 teaspoon baking powder

½ teaspoon salt

1 cup sour cream

⅓ cup hot (not boiling) water

Caramel bananas

2 tablespoons light corn syrup

3 tablespoons unsalted butter

2 tablespoons packed dark brown sugar

2 tablespoons heavy cream

2 ripe bananas, sliced

Banana cream

1 very ripe banana, mashed with the freshly squeezed juice of ½ a lemon

1¼ cups whipped heavy cream

12 dried banana chips

two 12-hole whoopie pie pans, greased (optional)

Makes 12

Preheat the oven to 350ºF.

To make the pies, mash the banana with the lemon juice in a bowl using a fork. Cream together the butter and sugar in a mixing bowl for 2–3 minutes using an electric handheld mixer, until light and creamy. Add the mashed banana and egg and mix again. Sift the flour and baking powder into the bowl and add the salt and sour cream. Whisk again until everything is incorporated. Add the hot water and whisk into the batter.

Put a large spoonful of batter into each hole in the prepared pans. (Alternatively, use 2 cookie sheets and follow the instructions given on page 7.) Leave to stand for 10 minutes then bake each pan in the preheated oven for 10–12 minutes. Remove the pies from the oven, let cool slightly then turn out onto a wire rack to cool completely.

To make the caramel bananas, gently heat the syrup, butter, and brown sugar in a saucepan until the sugar has dissolved and you have a smooth caramel sauce. Slowly pour in the heavy cream and stir until it is incorporated then remove from the heat and allow to cool. When cooled, remove a little sauce and reserve for decoration. Add the banana slices to the saucepan and toss gently using a spoon to ensure the banana slices are well coated.

To make the banana cream, fold the mashed banana into the whipped cream. Spoon some onto 12 of the pie halves, reserving enough to use as a topping. Add a spoonful of caramel bananas and cover with the remaining pie halves. Put a spoonful of the banana cream on top of each pie, add a dried banana chip and a drizzle of the reserved caramel sauce. Your whoopie pies are ready to enjoy.

rose and violet cream pies

I just adore rose and violet creams with their floral fondant fillings, rich bittersweet chocolate shells and crystalized rose and violet petal decorations. I have transferred all these elements to these dainty little pies for the most elegant of teatime treats or the perfect edible gift.

1 stick unsalted butter or vegetable shortening, softened

1 cup packed dark brown sugar

1 large egg

1 teaspoon vanilla extract

2 cups plus 2 tablespoons self-rising flour

⅓ cup cocoa powder

1 teaspoon baking powder

½ teaspoon salt

1 cup buttermilk

⅓ hot (not boiling) water

Rose and violet fillings

1 cup heavy cream

1 cup mascarpone cheese

2 tablespoons confectioners' sugar

1 tablespoon rose syrup

1 tablespoon violet syrup

pink and purple food colorings

To decorate

5½ oz. bittersweet chocolate

crystalized rose and violet petals

two cookie sheets, lined with baking parchment or silicone mats

a piping bag fitted with a large round nozzle (optional)

two piping bags, each fitted with a medium round nozzle

24 foil petit four cases

Makes 24

Preheat the oven to 350ºF.

To make the pies, cream together the butter and brown sugar in a mixing bowl for 2–3 minutes using an electric handheld mixer, until light and creamy. Add the egg and vanilla extract and mix again. Sift the flour, cocoa, and baking powder into the bowl and add the salt and buttermilk. Whisk again until everything is incorporated. Add the hot water and whisk into the batter.

Spoon the batter into the first prepared piping bag and pipe 48 rounds onto the prepared cookie sheets (about 1-inch diameter) leaving a gap between each pie as they will spread during baking. (Alternatively, use 2 teaspoons to form small rounds on the sheets.) Leave to stand for 10 minutes then bake each sheet in the preheated oven for 10–12 minutes. Remove from the oven, let cool slightly then transfer to a wire rack to cool.

To make the fillings, whip the heavy cream to stiff peaks. In a separate bowl, beat the mascarpone until softened then fold it into the whipped cream along with the confectioners' sugar. Transfer half of the mixture to a separate bowl; add the rose syrup and a few drops of pink food coloring to 1 bowl and the violet syrup and a drop of purple food coloring to the other. Mix both creams with an electric handheld mixer.

Spoon the fillings into the remaining prepared piping bags and pipe circles of each flavor onto 12 pie halves, so that you have 24 pie halves covered with cream. Top with the remaining pie halves. To decorate, melt the chocolate following the instructions given on page 10. Spoon a little melted chocolate on each pie, top with a crystalized rose or violet petal, as appropriate to the filling, and allow to set. Put them in petit four cases and your whoopie pies are ready to enjoy.

luxury pies

coconut cloud pies

Eating coconut always transports me to sunnier climes, especially with the addition of coconut rum! Sweetened soft shredded coconut (such as Baker's Angel Flake) works best due to its long strands but desiccated coconut also looks pretty if you are unable to find it.

1 stick unsalted butter or vegetable shortening, softened

1 cup packed dark brown sugar

1 large egg

2½ cups self-rising flour

1 teaspoon baking powder

½ teaspoon salt

1 cup sour cream

½ cup sweetened shredded coconut

⅓ cup hot (not boiling) water

Coconut mousse filling

7 oz. white chocolate

3 tablespoons coconut rum

1¼ cups heavy cream

½ cup sweetened shredded coconut

To decorate

3½ oz. white chocolate

⅔ cup sweetened shredded coconut

two 12-hole whoopie pie pans, greased (optional)

a piping bag fitted with a large round nozzle (optional)

Makes 12

Begin by preparing the coconut mousse filling as this needs to set in the fridge. Melt the white chocolate following the instructions on page 10 and allow to cool. Add the rum to the heavy cream and whip to stiff peaks. Fold in the melted chocolate and shredded coconut and chill in the fridge for 1–2 hours, until the mousse has set.

Preheat the oven to 350°F. To make the pies, cream together the butter and brown sugar in a mixing bowl for 2–3 minutes using a handheld electric mixer, until light and creamy. Add the egg and mix again. Sift the flour and baking powder into the bowl and add the salt, sour cream, and coconut. Whisk again until everything is incorporated. Add the hot water and whisk into the batter.

Put a large spoonful of batter into each hole in the prepared pans. (Alternatively, use 2 cookie sheets and follow the instructions given on page 7.) Let stand for 10 minutes then bake each pan in the preheated oven for 10–12 minutes. Remove from the oven, let cool slightly then turn out onto a wire rack to cool completely.

To decorate, melt the white chocolate following the instructions on page 10 and allow to cool. Pour the melted chocolate in a shallow dish and sprinkle the shredded coconut over a flat plate. Roll the sides of each pie half in the chocolate and then in the coconut. Return the pies to the wire rack and let the chocolate set.

Spoon the coconut mousse filling into the prepared piping bag and pipe circles of mousse onto 12 of the decorated pie halves. (If you do not have a piping bag, spread the filling over the pie halves with a round-bladed knife.) Top with the remaining pie halves and your whoopie pies are ready to enjoy.

grasshopper pies

These pies take their inspiration from the Grasshopper cocktail, made with mint, cocoa liqueur, and milk. I don't know anyone who doesn't delight in these classic after-dinner flavors.

1 stick unsalted butter or vegetable shortening, softened

1 cup packed dark brown sugar

1 large egg

1 teaspoon peppermint essence

2 cups plus 2 tablespoons self-rising flour

⅓ cup cocoa powder

1 teaspoon baking powder

½ teaspoon salt

½ cup sour cream

½ cup buttermilk

⅓ cup hot (not boiling) water

Mint mousse filling

10 oz. white chocolate

1 cup heavy cream

1 teaspoon peppermint essence

green food coloring

To decorate

7 oz. mint-flavored semisweet chocolate (not fondant-filled)

green sprinkles (balls or strands)

two 12-hole whoopie pie pans, greased (optional)

a piping bag fitted with a large round nozzle (optional)

Makes 12

Preheat the oven to 350ºF.

To make the pies, cream together the butter and brown sugar in a mixing bowl for 2–3 minutes using an electric handheld mixer, until light and creamy. Add the egg and peppermint essence and mix again. Sift the flour, cocoa, and baking powder into the bowl and add the salt, sour cream, and buttermilk. Whisk again until everything is incorporated. Add the hot water and whisk into the batter.

Put a large spoonful of batter into each hole in the prepared pans. (Alternatively, use 2 cookie sheets and follow the instructions given on page 7.) Let stand for 10 minutes then bake each pan in the preheated oven for 10–12 minutes. Remove from the oven, let cool slightly then turn out onto a wire rack to cool completely.

To make the mint mousse filling, melt the white chocolate following the instructions given on page 10 and set aside to cool. When the chocolate has cooled but is still runny, whip the heavy cream to stiff peaks. Pour in the cooled melted chocolate, add the peppermint essence and a few drops of green food coloring and whisk together. Cover and chill the mousse in the fridge for 1 hour.

Meanwhile, melt the mint-flavored chocolate following the instructions given on page 10. Spread it over the top of 12 of the pie halves using a round-bladed knife, scatter over some green sprinkles, and leave to set. Spoon the chilled mousse into the prepared piping bag and pipe blobs of the mousse onto the remaining pie halves. (If you do not have a piping bag, spread the filling over the pie halves with a round-bladed knife.) Top with the decorated pie halves and your whoopie pies are ready to enjoy.

almond and amaretto pies

1 stick unsalted butter or vegetable
shortening, softened

1 cup packed dark brown sugar

1 egg

1 teaspoon almond essence

2 cups plus 2 tablespoons
self-rising flour

1 teaspoon baking powder

½ cup ground almonds

½ teaspoon salt

1 cup sour cream

1 tablespoon amaretto liqueur

⅓ cup hot (not boiling) water

Amaretto cream

1¼ cups heavy cream

3 tablespoons amaretto liqueur

To decorate

6 oz. white chocolate

6–7 amaretti cookies, crumbled

two 12-hole whoopie pie pans,
greased (optional)

a piping bag fitted with a large
star nozzle (optional)

Makes 12

Amaretto is an Italian liqueur made from apricot kernels. These whoopie pies pay homage to this delicious drink with a delicate almond flavor and a crisp amaretti cookie and white chocolate coating. Serve with a glass of amaretto on ice for a special treat.

Preheat the oven to 350°F.

To make the pies, cream together the butter and brown sugar in a mixing bowl for 2–3 minutes using an electric handheld mixer, until light and creamy. Add the egg and almond essence and mix again. Sift the flour and baking powder into the bowl and add the ground almonds, salt, sour cream, and amaretto. Whisk again until everything is incorporated. Add the hot water and whisk into the batter.

Put a large spoonful of batter into each hole in the prepared pans. (Alternatively, use 2 cookie sheets and follow the instructions given on page 7.) Let stand for 10 minutes then bake each pan in the preheated oven for 10–12 minutes. Remove from the oven, let cool slightly then turn out onto a wire rack to cool completely.

To decorate the pies, melt the white chocolate following the instructions given on page 10. Sprinkle the amaretti crumbs over a plate and pour the melted chocolate into a shallow dish. Roll the sides of all the pie halves in the chocolate and then roll again in the amaretti crumbs. Return to the wire rack to set. Using a fork, drizzle the tops of 12 of the pie halves with the leftover white chocolate.

To make the amaretto cream filling, put the heavy cream and amaretto in a mixing bowl and whip to stiff peaks. Spoon into the prepared piping bag and pipe stars of filling onto the 12 pie halves that are not decorated with chocolate on top. (If you do not have a piping bag, spread the filling over the pie halves with a round-bladed knife.) Top with the decorated pie halves and your whoopie pies are ready to enjoy.

gingerbread pies

These pies, inspired by the German soft iced gingerbread Lebkuchen, are a perfect winter treat. If serving as part of your holiday celebrations, why not let your imagination run wild with the decoration and top the pies with snowy, winter wonderland scenes. If you can't find royal icing sugar, substitute with confectioners' sugar and add 1 tablespoon of egg white.

Begin by soaking the sultanas in the gingerbread liqueur (if using) for several hours, so that they become plump and juicy.

Preheat the oven to 350ºF. To make the pies, cream together the butter and brown sugar in a mixing bowl for 2–3 minutes using an electric handheld mixer, until light and creamy. Add the egg, golden raisins, and their soaking liquid and mix again. Sift the flour, baking powder, cinnamon, apple pie spice, and ginger into the bowl and add the salt and sour cream. Whisk again until everything is incorporated. Add the hot water and whisk into the batter.

Put a large spoonful of batter into each hole in the prepared pans. (Alternatively, use 2 cookie sheets and follow the instructions given on page 7.) Leave to stand for 10 minutes then bake each pan in the preheated oven for 10–12. Remove from the oven, let cool slightly then turn out onto a wire rack to cool completely.

To make the icing, whisk the royal icing sugar with ⅓ cup cold water for about 5 minutes, until the icing is very stiff. Put a tablespoonful of icing on 12 of the pie halves and use a fork to form it into sharp peaks. Arrange a ring of white balls around the outside edge then add a reindeer or Christmas tree to each pie. Leave to set.

To make the ginger cream filling, whisk together the butter, sour cream, confectioners' sugar, and gingerbread syrup using an electric handheld mixer, until light and creamy. Spoon the filling into the prepared piping bag and pipe a swirl onto the un-iced pie halves. (If you don't have a piping bag, spread the filling over the pie halves with a round-bladed knife.) Top with the iced pie halves and your whoopie pies are ready to enjoy.

⅓ cup golden raisins

¼ cup gingerbread liqueur (optional)

1 stick unsalted butter or vegetable shortening, softened

1 cup packed light brown sugar

1 large egg

2½ cups self-rising flour

1 teaspoon baking powder

2 teaspoons ground cinnamon

1 teaspoon apple pie spice

1 teaspoon ground ginger

1 cup sour cream

½ teaspoon salt

⅓ cup hot (not boiling) water

Ginger cream filling

1 stick unsalted butter

3 tablespoons sour cream

2¾ cups confectioners' sugar

3 tablespoons gingerbread syrup (such as Monin's Pain d'Epices)

Decoration

3⅔ cups royal icing sugar

white or silver balls (dragees)

reindeer and/or Christmas trees

two 12-hole whoopie pie pans, greased (optional)

a piping bag fitted with a large star nozzle (optional)

Makes 12

ice cream pies

These pies are a classic chocolate whoopie, just a little bit chillier, and perfect for a barbecue party on a summer's day. You'll need to assemble them at the last minute so that the ice cream doesn't melt. I've used vanilla here but you can substitute any flavor you like—why not try chocolate for a double chocolate treat!

1 stick unsalted butter or vegetable shortening, softened

1 cup packed dark brown sugar

1 large egg

1 teaspoon vanilla extract

2 cups plus 2 tablespoons self-rising flour

⅓ cup cocoa powder

1 teaspoon baking powder

½ teaspoon salt

1 cup plain yogurt

⅓ cup hot (not boiling) water

Ice cream filling

14 oz. vanilla ice cream in a block

multicolored sprinkles, to decorate

two 12-hole whoopie pie pans, greased (optional)

a 3-inch round cookie cutter

Makes 12

Preheat the oven to 350ºF.

To make the pies, cream together the butter and brown sugar in a mixing bowl for 2–3 minutes using an electric handheld mixer, until light and creamy. Add the egg and vanilla extract and mix again. Sift the flour, cocoa, and baking powder into the bowl and add the salt and yogurt. Whisk again until everything is incorporated. Add the hot water and whisk into the batter.

Put a large spoonful of batter into each hole in the prepared pans. (Alternatively, use 2 cookie sheets and follow the instructions given on page 7.) Leave to stand for 10 minutes then bake the pies in the preheated oven for 10–12 minutes. Remove from the oven, let cool slightly then turn out onto a wire rack to cool completely.

Shortly before you are ready to serve, remove the ice cream from the ice box and allow to soften slightly. Cut 12 slices each about 1-inch thick and, using the cookie cutter, stamp out a round from each slice. Sandwich an ice cream round between 2 cooled pie halves. Working quickly, put the sprinkles on a flat plate and roll each pie in them so that the ice cream is coated. Serve your whoopie pies immediately with paper napkins to catch any ice cream drips.

party
pies

valentine heart pies

As a special treat for loved ones on Valentine's Day, why not make these pretty pies. With strawberries, cherries, cranberries, white chocolate chips, and a pink chocolate glaze, what could be a more romantic way of showing you care?

1 stick unsalted butter or vegetable shortening, softened
1 cup granulated sugar
1 large egg
1 teaspoon vanilla extract
2½ cups self-rising flour
1 teaspoon baking powder
½ teaspoon salt
1 cup plain yogurt
⅓ cup dried cranberries
⅓ dried dried tart cherries
⅓ white chocolate chips
⅓ cup hot (not boiling) water

Strawberry cream filling
1½ cups fresh strawberries
2 tablespoons granulated sugar
freshly squeezed juice of ½ a lemon
1¼ cups heavy cream

Pink chocolate glaze
5½ oz. white chocolate
¼ cup corn syrup
1 tablespoon unsalted butter
a few drops of pink food coloring
assorted heart-shaped sprinkles, to decorate

two 6-hole heart-shaped cupcake pans, greased (optional)
a piping bag fitted with a large star nozzle (optional)

Makes 12

Preheat the oven to 350ºF.

To make the pies, cream together the butter and sugar in a mixing bowl for 2–3 minutes using an electric handheld mixer, until light and creamy. Add the egg and vanilla extract and mix again. Sift the flour and baking powder into the bowl and add the salt, yogurt, cranberries, cherries, and chocolate chips. Mix again until everything is incorporated. Add the hot water and whisk into the batter.

Put a large spoonful of batter into each hole in the prepared pans. (Alternatively, use 2 cookie sheets and follow the instructions given on page 7, but piping the mixture into heart shapes.) Leave to stand for 10 minutes then bake each pan in the preheated oven for 10–12 minutes. Remove from the oven, let cool slightly then turn out onto a wire rack to cool completely.

To make the filling, put the strawberries, sugar, and lemon juice in a small saucepan and add ¼ cup cold water. Simmer over low heat, until the strawberries are very soft. Purée until smooth in a blender and set aside to cool. Whip the heavy cream to stiff peaks then fold in the cooled strawberry purée. Chill in the fridge until required.

To make the pink chocolate glaze, put the white chocolate, corn syrup, butter, and 2 tablespoons cold water in a bowl and set over a pan of simmering water. Heat until the chocolate has melted and you have a smooth syrup. Add the pink food coloring. Spoon the glaze over 12 of the pie halves, wait 5 minutes then spoon over a second coat. This is best done whilst the pies are still on the wire rack and with baking parchment underneath to catch any drips. Sprinkle with sugar hearts and leave to set.

Spoon the strawberry cream filling into the prepared piping bag and pipe a generous swirl of cream onto the unglazed pie halves. (If you don't have a piping bag, spread the filling over the pie halves with a round-bladed knife.) Top each one with a glazed pie half. Your whoopie pies are now ready to enjoy.

whoopie croquembouche

This is the ultimate celebration of the wonderful whoopie pie, a giant stack of pies inspired by the French tower of choux buns known as a croquembouche. A perfect centerpiece for a party or even a wedding, as you can make the pies any color you wish to fit in with your color scheme.

4 sticks unsalted butter or vegetable shortening, softened

4 cups granulated sugar

4 large eggs

4 teaspoon vanilla extract

10 cups self-rising flour

4 teaspoons baking powder

2 teaspoons salt

2 cups buttermilk

2 cups sour cream

1⅔ cups hot (not boiling) water

red, orange, yellow, green, blue, and purple food colorings

Buttercream filling

3 sticks unsalted butter, softened

12 cups confectioners' sugar, sifted

¾ cup milk

2 teaspoons vanilla extract

eight 12-hole whoopie pie pans, greased (or you can cook in batches if you do not have enough pans or cookie sheets)

a piping bag fitted with a large star nozzle (optional)

a cone made with thin cardboard 10-in diameter and 10-in tall

thin ribbons in various colours

a long metal skewer with a ring

Makes 1 croquembouche (47 individual pies)

Preheat the oven to 350ºF.

To make the pies, cream together the butter and sugar in a very large mixing bowl for 2–3 minutes using an electric handheld mixer, until light and creamy. (Because of the large quantities required, you may prefer to make the mixture up in 2 batches.) Add the eggs and vanilla extract and mix again. Sift the flour and baking powder into the bowl and add the salt, buttermilk, and sour cream. Whisk again until everything is incorporated. Add the hot water and whisk into the batter.

Divide the mixture into 6 separate bowls ready for coloring, allowing a heaping tablespoon of mixture for each whoopie pie half. Add food coloring to make 10 red, 12 orange, 14 yellow, 16 green, 20 blue, and 22 purple pie halves. Place a large spoonful of mixture into each hole in the prepared pans. (Alternatively, use 4 cookie sheets and follow the instructions given on page 7.) Leave to stand for 10 minutes then bake each pan in the preheated oven for 10–12 minutes. Remove from the oven, let cool slightly then turn out on a wire rack to cool completely.

To make the buttercream filling, whisk together the butter, confectioners' sugar, milk, and vanilla extract until light and creamy. Spoon into the prepared piping bag and pipe a swirl between each pair of pies. (If you do not have a piping bag, spread the filling over the pie halves with a round-bladed knife.) Reserve a little of the buttercream.

To assemble the tower, begin by cutting the top off of the prepared cardboard cone to remove the point. Place the cone on a cake stand or similar and fix in place with the reserved buttercream. Put the purple pies around the base of the cone and the repeat with the remaining colors until your tower is assembled. Tie the ribbons to the ring of the skewer and push it through the pie at the top of the tower. Lower the skewer into the top open end of the cone to secure the top pie. Arrange the ribbons around the tower and your whoopie pie croquembouche is now ready to dazzle!

giant birthday whoopie pie

What could be more fun than celebrating a birthday with this oversized whoopie pie? The recipe has a rich chocolate glaze, classic marshmallow fluff filling and fresh strawberries and you can finish it with candles and any decorations that you like.

1 stick unsalted butter or vegetable shortening, softened

1 cup packed dark brown sugar

1 large egg

1 teaspoon vanilla extract

2 cups plus 2 tablespoons self-rising flour

⅓ cup cocoa powder

1 teaspoon baking powder

½ teaspoon salt

1 cup sour cream

⅓ cup hot (not boiling) water

Marshmallow fluff filling

a 7½-oz jar marshmallow fluff

1 stick unsalted butter, softened

1⅔ cups confectioners' sugar

1 teaspoon vanilla extract

3 tablespoons milk

1 generous cup fresh strawberries, hulled and halved

Chocolate frosting

1¼ cup confectioners' sugar

¼ cup cocoa powder

white and semisweet chocolate curls, rice paper (wafer) flowers, sprinkles, and candles, to decorate

2 large cookie sheets, greased and lined with baking parchment

a piping bag fitted with a large star nozzle (optional)

Serves 10-12

Preheat the oven to 350°F.

To make the pies, cream together the butter and brown sugar in a mixing bowl for 2–3 minutes using an electric handheld mixer, until light and creamy. Add the egg and vanilla extract and mix again. Sift the flour, cocoa, and baking powder into the bowl and add the salt and sour cream. Whisk again until everything is incorporated. Add the hot water and whisk into the batter.

Divide the batter between the prepared cookie sheets and spread each out into a 9-inch circle. Leave to stand for 10 minutes then bake each sheet in the preheated oven for 12–15 minutes. Remove from the oven and let cool completely on the cookie sheets.

To make the filling, whisk together the marshmallow fluff and butter using an electric handheld mixer. Sift in the confectioners' sugar, add the vanilla extract and milk and whisk again for 3–5 minutes, until light and creamy. Spoon the filling into the prepared piping bag. Put one of the pie halves on a cake stand and pipe a row of stars around the outside edge, alternating with the strawberries. Pipe the remaining filling in a continuous swirl, working towards the center of the pie base. Top with the remaining strawberries and put the other pie half on top. (If you don't have a piping bag, spread the filling over the pie half with a round-bladed knife and put the strawberries on top.)

To make the chocolate frosting, mix the confectioners' sugar, cocoa powder, and 2 tablespoons cold water to a smooth paste. Spread over the top of the pie and decorate as desired. Allow the frosting to set and your whoopie pie is ready to enjoy.

flamingo pies

1 stick unsalted butter or vegetable shortening, softened
1 cup granulated sugar
1 large egg
1 teaspoon pink food coloring
1 teaspoon vanilla extract
2½ cups self-rising flour
1 teaspoon baking powder
½ teaspoon salt
1 cup buttermilk
⅓ cup hot (not boiling) water

Pink cream filling
½ teaspoon pink food coloring
1¼ cups heavy cream

Frosting and decoration
1⅔ cups confectioners' sugar
pink and orange food coloring
1 teaspoon vanilla extract
½ cup sweetened soft shredded coconut (such as Baker's Angel Flakes)

edible glitter and sparkles

two 12-hole whoopie pie pans, greased (optional)

Makes 12

These are the pinkest of pies. I served these at an "Alice in Wonderland" themed tea party in honor of the flamingo croquet match played between Alice and the Queen of Hearts. Serve decorated with pink feathers for the ultimate flamingo fandango!

Preheat the oven to 350ºF.

To make the pies, cream together the butter and sugar in a mixing bowl for 2–3 minutes using an electric handheld mixer, until light and creamy. Add the egg, pink food coloring, and vanilla extract and mix again. Sift the flour and baking powder into the bowl and add the salt and buttermilk. Whisk again until everything is incorporated. Add the hot water and whisk into the batter.

Put a large spoonful of mixture into each hole in the prepared pans. (Alternatively, use 2 cookie sheets and follow the instructions given on page 7.) Leave to stand for 10 minutes then bake each pan in the preheated oven for 10–12 minutes. Remove from the oven, let cool slightly then turn out onto a wire rack to cool completely.

To make the frosting, mix the confectioners' sugar, 2–3 teaspoons cold water, a few drops of pink food coloring, and the vanilla extract to a smooth paste. Divide the shredded coconut between 2 bowls; add pink food coloring to 1 and orange food coloring to the other and mix until colored. Spoon the pink frosting over 12 of the pie halves. This is best done whilst the pies are still on the wire rack, with baking parchment underneath to catch any drips. Sprinkle with the pink and orange shredded coconut and dust with glitter and sparkles. Allow the frosting to set.

To make the pink cream filling, add a few drops of pink food coloring to the heavy cream and whip to stiff peaks. Put a spoonful of filling on top of the 12 un-iced pie halves and spread with a round-bladed knife. Top with the iced pie halves and your whoopie pies are ready to enjoy.

oyster pies

1 stick unsalted butter or vegetable shortening, softened

1 cup granulated sugar

1 egg

1 teaspoon vanilla extract

2½ cups self-rising flour

1 teaspoon baking powder

½ teaspoon salt

½ cup plain yogurt

½ cup sour cream

⅓ cup hot (not boiling) water

Filling and decoration

7 tablespoons confectioners' sugar

3–4 tablespoons marshmallow fluff

white sprinkles (ideally tiny balls)

1¾ cups heavy cream

10 sugar pearls

10 oz. graham crackers or digestive biscuits (optional)

two 6-hole shell-shaped baking pans, greased

a piping bag fitted with a small round nozzle

a piping bag fitted with a large star nozzle

Makes 12

Served on cookie crumb "sand", these amusing pies are perfect for any beach-themed party. You will need a baking pan with shell-shaped molds, as it's not possible to create the shape by any other means. Bake in batches if you can only find one pan.

Preheat the oven to 350°F.

To make the pies, cream together the butter and sugar in a mixing bowl for 2–3 minutes using an electric handheld mixer, until light and creamy. Add the egg and vanilla extract and mix again. Sift the flour and baking powder into the bowl and add the salt, yogurt, and sour cream. Whisk again until everything is incorporated. Add the hot water and whisk into the batter.

Put a large spoonful of batter into each hole in the prepared pans. Leave to stand for 10 minutes then bake the pies in the preheated oven for 10–12 minutes. Remove the pies from the oven, let cool slightly and then turn out onto cool on a wire rack to cool completely.

To decorate, mix the confectioners' sugar and 2–3 teaspoons cold water to a thick smooth paste. Spoon the frosting into the piping bag fitted with a small round nozzle and pipe fine lines on top of 12 of the pie halves, as shown. Use a round-bladed knife to spread a little marshmallow fluff around the front edges of the iced pie halves and roll them in the sprinkles to decorate. Set aside.

To make the "seafoam" filling, whip the cream to stiff peaks then spoon into it the piping bag fitted with a large star nozzle. Pipe lines of cream onto the undecorated pie halves, as shown, and add a sugar pearl. Top each one with a decorated pie half.

Crush the cookies, if using, in a food processor or put them in a polythene bag and bash with a rolling pin to make fine crumbs. Sprinkle over a serving plate or tray and place your oyster pies on top of the "sand". Your whoopie pies are now ready to enjoy.

index

almond and amaretto pies 48
apple crumble pies 33

bananas: banoffee pies 41
birthday whoopie pie 59
buttercream: chocolate 10
  vanilla 13
  whoopie croquembouche 56
buttermilk: apple crumble pies
  33
  caramel popcorn pies 26
  classic whoopie pie 9
  cookies and cream pies 22
  flamingo pies 60
  grasshopper pies 46
  key lime jello pies 37
  lemon sherbet pies 35
  peanut butter and jelly pies
  18
  red velvet pies 10
  rose and violet cream pies 42
  strawberry cream pies 30
  vanilla dream 13
  whoopie croquembouche 56

caramel: banoffee pies 41
  caramel popcorn pies 26
Chambord raspberry pies 38
cherries: chocolate and cherry
  pies 29
  Valentine heart pies 55
chocolate: apple crumble pies
  33
  chocolate and cherry pies 29
  classic whoopie pie 9
  coconut cloud pies 45
  cookies and cream pies 22
  giant birthday whoopie pie 59
  grasshopper pies 46
  mocha pies 14
  red velvet pies 10
  Valentine heart pies 55
classic whoopie pie 9
coconut: coconut cloud pies 45
  flamingo pies 60
coffee: mocha pies 14
cookies and cream pies 22
cranberries: Valentine heart pies
  55
cream: almond and amaretto
  pies 48
  banoffee pies 41

Chambord raspberry pies 38
coconut cloud pies 45
custard filling 33
flamingo pies 60
rose and violet cream pies 42
strawberry cream pies 30
Valentine heart pies 55
  see also sour cream
cream cheese: key lime jello
  pies 37
  lemon sherbet pies 35
  pumpkin pies 17
croquembouche, whoopie 56
crumble topping 33
custard filling 33

flamingo pies 60

giant birthday whoopie pie 59
gingerbread pies 50–1
glacé icing: coffee 14
  lemon 35
  lime 37
glazes: caramel 26
  Chambord 38
  chocolate 29, 59
  maple 25
  peanut 18
  pink chocolate 55
grasshopper pies 46

ice cream pies 52

key lime jello pies 37

lemon sherbet pies 35
lime: key lime jello pies 37

maple syrup: pecan pies 25
marshmallow fluff: classic
  whoopie pie 9
  giant birthday whoopie pie
  59
  oyster pies 63
mascarpone cheese: Chambord
  raspberry pies 38
  rose and violet cream pies 42
meringue filling 21
mini pistachio pies 21
mint: grasshopper pies 46
mocha pies 14

oyster pies 63

peanut butter and jelly pies 18
pecan pies 25

peppermint: grasshopper pies
  46
pistachio pies, mini 21
popcorn pies, caramel 26
praline cream filling 25
pumpkin pies 17

raspberries: Chambord
  raspberry pies 38
raspberry jam: peanut butter
  and jelly pies 18
red velvet pies 10
rose and violet pies: rose and violet
  cream pies 42
rose syrup: rose and violet
  cream pies 42
  strawberry cream pies 30
rum: coconut cloud pies 45

salted caramel sauce 26
sour cream: almond and
  amaretto pies 48
  banoffee pies 41
  classic whoopie pie 9
  coconut cloud pies 45
  cookies and cream pies 22
  giant birthday whoopie pie
  59
  gingerbread pies 50–1
  grasshopper pies 46
  key lime jelly pies 37
  mocha pies 14
  oyster pies 63
  pecan pies 25
  vanilla dream 13
  whoopie croquembouche 56
strawberries: giant birthday
  whoopie pie 59
  strawberry cream pies 30
  Valentine heart pies 55
sultanas: gingerbread pies
  50–1

Valentine heart pies 55
vanilla dream 13
violet syrup: rose and violet
  cream pies 42

whoopie croquembouche 56
whoopie pie, classic 9

yogurt: chocolate and cherry
  pies 29
  ice cream pies 52
  mini pistachio pies 21
  oyster pies 63
  pumpkin pies 17
  strawberry cream pies 30
  Valentine heart pies 55

Author's Acknowledgments

As ever, a huge thank you to wonderful Ryland Peters & Small for publishing this book, and in particular Julia Charles for knowing that I was a "whoopie pie kind of gal" and for doing such a kind and patient job editing my recipes. Steve Painter for the wonderful styling and photographs and for going beyond the call of duty to find pink flamingo feathers. Maxine Clark, a kindred spirit, for the beautiful food styling—you transformed my little pies into elegant delights! Heather and Elly at HHB, two very special people who guide me every step of the way. Sacha, Mum, Mike, Dad, Liz, Gareth, Amy, Jane, Geoff, and the Patel family for always being there and for loving me even when I make a mess in the kitchen. My tasters who ate their way through almost 500 pies (may your waistlines forgive me someday); David, Lucy, Kathie, Jess, Miles, Josh, Rosie, Tina, Maren, Alison, Ella, Torin, Peter, Susan, Pauline, Steven, Tena, Pete, Pam, Steve, Ed, Kate, and Thomas.